Write to Publish

Teaching Writing Skills Through Classroom Magazine Publishing

Written by
Kristin K. Hildum

Editors
Joanne Corker and Karen P. Hall

Illustrator
Corbin Hillam

Project Director
Carolea Williams

Table of Contents

Mini-Lessons 49

Reproducibles 73

Appendix 128

Introduction

Write to Publish contains everything you need to implement a successful writing program in your classroom. Students become part of a classroom publishing workforce, practicing real-life writing skills as they produce magazines for peers, friends, and family to enjoy.

Students participate in every step of the publishing process. They are both writers and editors, receiving official titles and training sessions to carry out specific jobs for the class "publishing house." They work together to write and edit articles, conduct staff meetings, and make group decisions about magazine content, layout, and distribution. Incentive plans are offered to reward students for performance and participation.

Student writing skills are developed and reinforced through whole-group mini-lessons, small-group sessions, peer tutoring, and one-on-one teacher conferencing. Every week, students participate in daily 45- to 60-minute writing activities. Reproducible guides and check-off lists help students edit and correct their own work, as well as assist others during the writing process.

As teacher, you play the role of Senior Editor, interviewing and training students for their jobs. You circulate, supervise, monitor, and advise students as they write and edit their work for publication.

Write to Publish has been used successfully with students of all backgrounds and abilities. Students actively participate in the writing process—they anticipate and are excited about writing, resulting in more on-task behavior and greater student productivity. Students show significant growth as they participate in the program, improving their writing and editing skills, developing greater self-esteem, and learning the true meaning of teamwork.

Program Outline

Magazine publishing may be incorporated into your curriculum any time in the school year. The following outline is based on a nine-week program with daily 45- to 60-minute writing sessions. Time requirements may vary depending on individual class schedules and student needs. Reproducible pages are indicated in parenthesis.

Setting the Stage

- Set up the classroom environment (pages 74–79).
- Collect materials and supplies.
- Tell parents about *Write to Publish* and recruit volunteers.
- Invite guest speakers to talk to students.
- Complete Interest Surveys (pages 80–81).

Assigning and Training Editorial Staff (1 week)*

- Review Job Descriptions (page 82).
- Fill out Job Applications (page 83).
- Conduct interviews.
- Assign staff positions and sign Job Contracts (page 84).
- Discuss and review the Editing Guide and Editors' Checklists (pages 86–90).
- Train editorial groups while others work on writing (pages 91–98).
- Distribute and collect subscription requests from other classes (page 85).

Writing Magazine Articles (3–4 weeks)*

- Create a class list of article formats.
- Guide students as they select article topics.
- Teach writing skills through mini-lessons (pages 104–113).
- Allot time for independent writing sessions.
- Conference with students and record student progress (pages 114–118).

Students as Editors (2–3 weeks)*

- Teach students to self-edit (pages 99–103, 119–121).
- Review the role of peer editors.
- Peer-edit using rotation stations, checklists, and sign-off sheets.
- Conference with students and record student progress.

Final Publication (2–3 weeks)*

- Guide students as they revise and rewrite final drafts.
- Add student-generated artwork and illustrations to the magazine.
- Review the roles of Art, Cover, and Layout Editors.
- Conduct staff meetings.
- Determine final art and layout of the magazine interior and cover.
- Print the magazine.
- Distribute the magazine to school and family members.

Post Production (2–3 days)

- Share student work and evaluate workshop success (page 122).
- Celebrate with a class party.
- Distribute rewards—certificates and "paychecks" (pages 123–127).
- Evaluate student success with teacher records.

* Job training, writing, and editing sessions overlap—students write while classmates receive training and begin the editing process.

Setting the Stage

Before beginning your writing program, it is important to set the stage for magazine publishing and give your students a "sneak preview" of what's to come. This chapter offers suggestions for classroom environment, organizing materials and supplies, and eliciting help from parent volunteers. Also included are prewriting activities to motivate and excite your students about writing through magazine publishing.

Classroom Environment

Just a few simple features are needed to change your classroom into an interactive publishing house. Use the following suggestions to create a working atmosphere that is both exciting and inviting to your students.

- Use your regular classroom seating arrangement for independent and partner work. Desks may be arranged individually, in pairs, or in groups of four. You may choose to designate specific areas as "quiet work stations."

- Designate one or two large work tables for small-group conferences, training sessions, and editorial meetings. Be certain that conference areas are positioned away from quiet work areas.

- Dedicate a bulletin board to student work at different stages of the publishing process. Invite students to decorate their own bulletin board, creating and displaying posters and decoratives for their publishing company.

- Create an inviting library corner with an assortment of children's magazines. Refer to the Appendix (page 128) for suggested titles and subscription addresses. Obtain old issues from your school or local library. Purchase cardboard display shelves from classroom supply stores, or check with card shops and drugstores for donations.

Sample Floor Plan

Bookshelves

Student Mailboxes

Beanbag

Classroom Library

Art Supplies

Bookshelves

Beanbag

Conference Table

Roller Cart with Reading Forms

Student Desks

Teacher Desk

Student Desks

Writing Materials

Student Desks

Paper/ Supplies

Storage

Student Desks

Computer and Printer

Bookshelves

Conference Table

Student Desks

Door

Files

Student Desks

Chalkboard

TV and VCR

Supplies

Many materials and supplies needed for this program can be found in your classroom or your school's supply room. Others are copies of reproducibles found on pages 74–127.

Publishing Supplies

Use hanging folders and storage crates for the following publishing supplies.

- Job name tags, placed inside plastic covers with pins (office supply stores) or laminated and threaded with yarn to form necklaces (pages 74–75)
- Job desk plates, laminated on tagboard for reuse (pages 76–79)
- Editors' Checklists, laminated for reuse (pages 87–90)
- Evaluation sheets—Writing Assessment, Editor's Grade Sheet/Rubric, Writer Evaluation, What I Learned About Magazine Publishing (pages 115, 117, 118, 122)
- Editor Sign-Off Sheets (page 103)

Student Folders

Use two-pocket, three-pronged folders to create student writing folders and file them in storage crates. Place the following materials in the *pronged section* of each folder.

- Job Descriptions (page 82)
- Job Contract (page 84)
- Editing Guide (page 86)
- Self-Editing Guide (page 99)
- Writer's Report (page 119)
- Article formats (class-generated list)

Place the following materials in the *pockets* of each folder.

- Writing pieces (brainstorming lists, rough drafts, edited copies, published work)
- Blank notebook paper
- Job name tag (job position assigned)
- Job desk plate (job position assigned)
- Editing checklist (job position assigned)

Student and Parent Involvement

After setting up your classroom environment and organizing supplies, add excitement by giving both students and parents a "sneak peak" at magazine publishing.

Student Motivation

Build curiosity and enthusiasm for the publishing process by completing the following pre-program activities with your students.

- Celebrate Magazine Madness Day. Invite students to bring magazines from home, or select magazines from the class library. Have them compare content, style, and layout of different magazines. Invite student pairs to rank magazines and individual articles from least to most favorite.

- Have students complete the Interest Survey. This generates curiosity about the publishing process and encourages students to think about their writing preferences. Surveys also provide you with an inventory of students' needs, attitudes, and capabilities.

- Connect classroom publishing to real-life experiences. Invite writers, editors, artists, and publishers to speak to your class.

- Invite students to tape-record or video-tape interviews. Have students interview writers, editors, artists, and publishers in your community and share results with the class.

- Invite students to learn more about the publishing process. Have students write letters to publishing houses requesting information about the publishing process, or visit a local publishing house to see professional publishing in action.

Parent Participation

Familiarize parents with the goals, components, and structure of the *Write to Publish* program through an Open House session or a parent newsletter. Have parent volunteers assist with the following tasks.

- Recruit guests to speak about the publishing business.
- Collect magazines and display shelves to create a class library.
- Donate publishing materials.
- Conduct student job interviews.
- Assist with magazine layout.
- Type revised student articles for final publication.
- Print and collate class magazines.
- Plan and organize the post-production party.

 # Dear Parents,

We are about to begin an exciting magazine publishing program in our classroom. Throughout this program, students are introduced to a wide variety of writing types and styles used in real life. Your child will participate in all phases of writing, from brainstorming to publishing. He or she will continually engage in writing that has an authentic purpose.

If you have any questions or are interested in assisting with this program, please let me know. We would appreciate help with:

- Recruiting guests to speak about the publishing business.
- Collecting magazines and display shelves to create a class library.
- Donating publishing materials.
- Conducting student job interviews.
- Assisting with magazine layout.
- Typing revised student articles for final publication.
- Printing and collating class magazines.
- Planning and organizing the post-production party.

This will be a very exciting and rewarding experience for everyone. I hope you will enjoy watching your child grow as a writer this year.

Sincerely,

✂ ---

Parent Volunteer Form

Parent Name _____

Please check off jobs in which you are interested.

❑ Recruiting guest speakers   ❑ Assisting with magazine layout
❑ Collecting used magazines   ❑ Typing student articles
❑ Donating publishing materials   ❑ Printing and collating the magazine
❑ Conducting interviews   ❑ Organizing a post-production party

Comments: _____

_____

Write to Publish © 1996 Creative Teaching Press

Classroom Management

Several steps of magazine publishing occur simultaneously, with students performing different tasks within one writing period. By previewing and planning materials in advance and using a few simple suggestions, you'll be amazed how smoothly each stage of magazine publishing progresses. This chapter provides practical guidelines to organize and manage instruction throughout the publishing process. Included are suggestions for day-to-day scheduling, nine-week program planning, student management tips, and ways to integrate writing across the curriculum.

Scheduling

Start magazine publishing any time prior to the last quarter of school. For best results, initiate the program at the beginning of the school year. Set aside a minimum of 45–60 minutes each day for magazine publishing. Writing periods may include a combination of one or more activities such as mini-lessons, independent writing sessions, and peer-editing. Flexibility is important—tailor the writing program to meet your students' needs.

Nine-Week Schedule

Use the following schedule to help you publish your first magazine. Note that many phases of magazine publishing occur simultaneously—students alternate between independent, partner, small-group, and whole-group activities. By organizing lessons in advance and setting clear goals for students, you ensure smooth transition from one phase of production to the next.

Week 1

Step 1 Give students and parents a "sneak preview" of the program. Decorate your classroom, set up writing files, and create a class library of magazines for students to explore. Send home parent letters explaining the goals of the program. Have students complete Interest Surveys in class or for homework.

Step 2 Have students brainstorm and vote on a magazine title. Ask them to compare and share components of different children's magazines to generate a class list of article formats (e.g., book reviews, poems).

Step 3 Assign students to staff positions. Use reproducibles to discuss editorial positions available, then have students fill out job applications. Conduct individual or group interviews during free periods or while other students write articles. Assign positions and have students sign contracts. If time permits, begin job training.

Step 4 Have Distribution Editors distribute and collect subscription order forms from other classes.

Week 2

Step 1 Teach a mini-lesson on nouns and adjectives (pages 50–51). Teach the whole class together, or instruct students in small groups while others write independently.

Step 2 Have students write articles. Ask students to use the class-generated list to choose a format for their articles. Help students brainstorm topic ideas. Have students store work in writing folders.

Step 3 Train editors in small groups. Use training samples and checklists to instruct editors how to edit work. Have other students write independently during training sessions. Take time to monitor and check writing progress in between training sessions.

Step 4 Conduct one-on-one or small-group conferences while other students work independently. Schedule two or three conferences a day, allowing time for you to circulate around the class and monitor seatwork.

Week 3

Step 1 Teach a mini-lesson on editing techniques (page 52).

Step 2 Teach students how to self-edit their work using guides and checklists. Have students self-edit work after their articles are complete.

Step 3 Allot one day for students to illustrate their work.

Step 4 Continue to conference with students and monitor progress.

Week 4

Step 1 Provide time for independent writing and self-editing. Encourage students to pace themselves, reminding them to do their best work.

Step 2 Choose and teach a mini-lesson based on students' needs.

Step 3 Have students begin peer-editing. Let students rotate freely, reminding them to respect those working around them. Set aside a quiet area for students to write and self-edit without distractions.

Step 4 Allot one day for students to illustrate their work.

Step 5 Continue to conference with students and monitor progress.

Week 5

Step 1 Provide time for independent writing and self-editing.

Step 2 Teach a mini-lesson.

Step 3 Have students continue peer-editing.

Step 4 Have students finish illustrations.

Step 5 Act as Senior Editor, checking papers edited by students.

Step 6 Continue to conference with students and monitor progress.

Week 6

Step 1 Teach a mini-lesson.

Step 2 Have students continue peer-editing.

Step 3 Check papers that have been peer-edited. Conference with the authors of these papers, and have students begin final revisions.

Step 4 Continue to conference with students and monitor progress.

Week 7

Step 1 Teach a mini-lesson.

Step 2 Have students finish peer-editing.

Step 3 Check edited papers and conference with the authors.

Step 4 Have students continue writing final revisions.

Step 5 Continue to conference with students and monitor progress.

Week 8

Step 1 Teach a mini-lesson.

Step 2 Review the roles of Art, Cover, and Layout Editors.

Step 3 Have students continue writing final article copies. Ask those that finish to submit articles to Layout Editors. If using parent volunteers to type final drafts for print, make copies of articles for Layout Editors as mock-ups while parents work with originals.

Step 4 Conduct staff meetings. Have Art, Cover, and Layout Editors begin work on final production.

Step 5 Monitor and guide progress of both independent and group activities.

Week 9

Step 1 Teach a mini-lesson. (You may choose to skip the mini-lesson during the last week and concentrate on the final steps of production.)

Step 2 Have students finish final article copies and submit them to Layout Editors.

Step 3 Have Art, Cover, and Layout Editors finish work on final production. Ask Layout Editors to make a mock-up layout for the whole class to review and approve before completing the final copy.

Step 4 Give writing assignments to students who are not part of Art, Cover, and Layout. Have them write on topics relating to past mini-lessons, or begin writing articles for the next magazine issue.

Step 5 Have Distribution Editors tally subscription forms. (Student volunteers may assist with this process.)

Step 6 Print magazine pages. Have students and/or parent volunteers collate and staple pages to create the final product. As students construct magazines, have them write addresses on the back and give to Distribution Editors to deliver to school subscribers.

Step 7 Evaluate and celebrate the completion of the magazine. Invite students to take magazines home to families and friends.

Sample Lesson Plan

Below is a sample lesson plan for the first week of magazine publishing. Use it as a guide to prepare your own daily schedules throughout the writing program.

Writing Schedule for Week 1

Monday
❶ Use children's magazines to introduce magazine publishing and discuss publishing issues (content, illustrations, layout).
❷ Have students complete Interest Surveys.
❸ Have student pairs skim through magazines and write lists of article formats.
❹ Generate a class list of article formats found in magazines.

Materials needed: children's magazines, Interest Surveys (pages 80–81), chart paper

---

Tuesday
❶ Brainstorm and select title and theme for the class magazine.
❷ Read through and discuss job descriptions.
❸ Have students write about and share jobs they would like to apply for and why.

Materials needed: Job Descriptions (page 82), writing paper

Wednesday
❶ Using an overhead, teach students how to complete job applications.
❷ Have students fill out job applications.
❸ Explain the interviewing process to students.

Materials needed: overhead projector, transparency, and Job Applications (page 83)

Thursday
❶ Present a mock interview for students.
❷ Interview students while others work independently (creating company business cards, promotional posters, free-choice writing).

Materials needed: completed Job Applications

Friday
❶ Announce job assignments, and have students sign Job Contracts.
❷ Have students use the class-generated list to begin writing articles.
❸ Discuss the Editing Guide and Editors' Checklists, and begin training editors while others work independently.

Materials needed: Job Contracts, Editing Guide, Editors' Checklists (pages 84, 86, 87–90)

Student Management

Consistent expectations and planning lessons in advance ensure smooth and successful completion of magazine publishing. Clearly outline goals and objectives for students before beginning each writing period. Provide backup activities for those who finish early. Emphasize the importance of cooperation and teamwork. Set up individual and group incentives to encourage independent and group achievement.

To Do List:
1. Finish writing your article.
2. Self-edit your work using the Self-Editing Guide.
3. Revise your paper.
4. Find a peer editor to edit your paper.
5. Finish illustrations for your article.

Keeping On Task

It is important to keep students occupied while you meet with small groups for training and conferencing. With many writing options and activities for students to choose from, off-task behavior is kept to a minimum. Activities may include brainstorming, creating writing webs, researching, writing articles, revising, and illustrating. Provide writing prompts for those students needing extra guidance, and list daily goals on the chalkboard to guide students as they work independently.

FRIENDSHIP
We all like having friends, but friendship is not always easy. Think of the time when you and a friend had a disagreement.

WRITING PROMPTS

Fostering Teamwork

Foster a "teamwork environment" as students work in groups. Invite students to brainstorm group rules, and post them in the classroom as an extension to your regular classroom rules. Some ideas may include:

- Take turns talking.
- Use quiet "group voices."
- Listen—all ideas are worth being heard.
- Never interrupt.
- Be considerate of your classmates and respect their ideas.
- If you disagree with a classmate, talk it out calmly.
- Don't waste time—you have a deadline.
- Remember, you are part of a team.

Rewards and Incentives

Set up an incentive plan, monitoring and rewarding students as they complete stages of the publishing process. Use "paychecks" and certificates (pages 123–127) to recognize student achievement. Reward students with a class party at the end of each issue, distributing their published work to share and enjoy.

Integrating Writing Across the Curriculum

Maximize classroom time by integrating writing with other subject areas such as literature, spelling, technology, and math. This helps students realize that school subjects and learning overlap in everyday life. The following ideas can help you connect writing to other subject areas.

Literature

Student-produced magazines provide readily-available, effective, and motivating reading materials. Students can read their articles aloud to small groups, partner-read their stories to younger grades, and participate in reader's theater. Encourage students to look for books in which characters write or tell stories (e.g., *Aunt Isabella Tells a Good One* by Kate Duke, *Dear Mr. Henshaw* by Beverly Cleary, and *The Jolly Postman* by Janet Ahlberg).

Spelling/Language

Have students search through their writing folders or personal dictionaries to find challenging or commonly misspelled words. Students may also select words from current reading material. Have them choose five to eight words each week, including more as achievement increases. Add five to ten of your own words to student lists. At the end of the week, test teacher-assigned words as a whole class, then have spelling partners check student-selected words.

Technology

Magazine publishing provides valuable, real-life opportunities for students to experiment and become familiar with computers and a variety of software. See your school's media specialist to find out what word processing, illustrating, and writing skills programs are available. Computer programs that work well include:

- *Amazing Animation* by Claris
- *The Children's Writing and Publishing Center* by The Learning Company
- *The Graph Club* by Tom Snyder
- *Kid Pix* by Broderbound
- *Print Shop* by Broderbound
- *Super Print* by Scholastic

Math

Show students that math and writing are interrelated in everyday life. Encourage them to incorporate math into magazine publishing using the following ideas.

Create math puzzles. Have students write directions, questions, and labels. Puzzles may include:

- *Maze Multiplication*—Place an assortment of numbers in a grid maze of sixteen boxes. Have the reader find the path from start to finish that multiplies to a specific product.
- *Finding 50*—Place numbers in a 36-square grid. Have the reader find groups of three number squares touching horizontally, vertically, or diagonally that add to 50.
- *Neighbors*—Draw a pattern of eight connecting squares. Have the reader write numerals *1–8* in the squares so that no number is vertically, horizontally, or diagonally next to the number that comes before or after it (e.g., two cannot be placed in a box next to one or three).

Make advertisements. Have students write prices, words, and phrases. Advertisements may include:

- Toys and games
- Movies playing at the local theater
- Lunchable munchables

Conduct surveys. Have students draw graphs and charts, tally numbers, and average values. Surveys may include:

- Total number of students in each grade level
- Average age of students in each class
- Total number of pets (dogs, cats, birds, fish)
- Colors of neighborhood cars

Assigning and Training Staff

The success of your publishing program depends on the extent of student involvement in the classroom workforce. Every student needs to feel he or she plays an important role in publishing the magazine. This chapter provides essential information about student "jobs" and how students apply and interview for them. You will also find suggestions for selecting and "hiring" your workforce and tips for training student editors.

TIME FRAME

Interviewing for and assigning jobs **3–4 days**

Training sessions **4–5 days**

Staff Positions

Use the Job Descriptions (page 82) to discuss staff positions. Explain that there will be several students assigned to each position. Depending on your class size, there may be four or five students with the same job title. Discuss that jobs will change with each new magazine, giving students the opportunity to perform various tasks throughout the year. Encourage students to first apply for jobs that match their capabilities, then branch out into other areas as the year progresses.

As the teacher, you are the Senior Editor. The Senior Editor interviews and trains students for their jobs and circulates, supervises, monitors, and conferences with student writers and editors. You make the final edit of the magazine, and evaluate writers, editors, and the magazine when it is finished.

Job Applications

Use an overhead projector and transparencies to guide students as they fill out Job Applications (page 83). Discuss how applications are used by employers to choose qualified candidates. Explain that employers look at neatness and accuracy as well as past experience when evaluating job applications. Show teacher-generated samples of well-written and poorly-written job applications for students to compare and evaluate.

Have students complete their own applications. You may choose to have students work independently or with a partner. Ask each student to apply for two different jobs, giving you flexibility when assigning positions. When finished, invite students to examine and compare real job descriptions and applications from local businesses.

Job Interviews

Before you interview, sort and group applications by first-choice positions. If too many students have selected the same positions, sort by second choices or ask for volunteers to fill vacancies.

Choose one of the following methods to interview students. Select the method that works best with your schedule.

Writing Time Interviews—Give individual interviews during independent writing time.

Panel Interviews—Talk with an entire group at a time, such as all students wishing to be Spelling Editors.

Adult Interviews—Ask parent volunteers or a teacher's assistant to interview students.

Recess Interviews—Interview students during recess.

Listening Center Interviews—Have students independently complete a tape-recorded interview at a listening center. Ask each student to say his or her name, date, and desired position. Have written questions next to the tape recorder for students to answer.

Presentation Interviews—Invite each student to prepare a brief statement to present to the entire class, explaining why he or she would be good at a particular position. Then he or she can answer questions from the class.

Ask students to work on free-choice or assigned writing topics when not being interviewed, or have them observe others going through the process. Keep interviews short (five minutes). Have students elaborate on answers from their applications.

Ask student volunteers to demonstrate the interviewing process before conducting real interviews—the more realistic the interviews, the more students enjoy them. Interview questions may include:

- *For which positions are you applying? Why?*
- *What editing experience do you have?*
- *What qualifications do you have for this job?*
- *What makes you the best person for this job?*

Job Placement

Announce job placements after interviewing is complete. Evaluating student needs and your own good judgement are the best determining factors for assigning student jobs. For the first issue, you may choose to place students in positions for which they are well qualified to build self-confidence. Make sure to emphasize the importance of all positions.

Students rarely become concerned about assigned jobs—you can usually accommodate one of their choices. They know they can apply for a different job next issue.

Have students sign Job Contracts (page 84) and keep them in their writing folders. Use the Student Editor Positions chart (page 116) to track jobs assigned throughout the year. You may choose to date each student's job and monitor selections to ensure each student occupies a variety of publishing positions throughout the year.

Student Editor Positions

Student Names	Art	Capitalization	Content	Cover	Distribution	Layout	Punctuation	Spelling
Anthony			1/15		9/27			
Jenna	9/27					1/15		

Training Staff

Train specific groups of editors (e.g., Content Editors) while others write independently. Use reproducible guides, checklists, and training samples to discuss and teach proper editing techniques. Use an overhead projector and transparencies to show samples of edited work.

Training Materials

Provide your students with the following materials:

- Editing Guide (page 86)—a list of conventional editing marks.
- Editors' Checklists (pages 87–90)—specific checklists to guide Capitalization, Content, Punctuation, and Spelling Editors for peer-editing.
- Training Samples (pages 91–98)—unedited writing samples to practice editing for capitalization, content, punctuation, and spelling.

Practice Sessions

Have students practice their editing skills with training samples and the appropriate editor's checklist. Remind students to complete only the specific editing jobs assigned (e.g., Content Editors edit for content only). Correct training samples and redistribute for students to check the accuracy of their work.

Role play with editors to demonstrate how to interact with others during peer-editing. Reinforce the importance of discussion between author and editor. Encourage editors to pace themselves and do careful work, editing no more than two papers in one class period. Emphasize the importance of positive feedback and instruct students to highlight errors but not rewrite papers— their role is to guide and encourage authors as they revise their own work.

After training is complete, hand out name tags and desk plates. Have students keep them in their writing folders when not in use. Refer to *Students as Editors* (pages 35–38) for specific guidelines on how to incorporate peer-editing into writing sessions.

Teaching Tips

- Invite more advanced students to write resumes as part of their job applications.
- Invite parents to watch the interviewing process. Video-tape interviews for students to view and self-assess.
- Make transparencies of edited work using commonly-known poems and stories. Rewrite sections of favorite stories such as *The Three Little Pigs* or *Hansel and Gretal* with errors, then show how editing marks are used to indicate corrections.
- Invite students to work in pairs when first training for their positions, or have partners exchange papers to check for accuracy.
- Have students generate a list of positive, constructive comments to use with authors during peer-editing.

Students as Writers

Students enjoy writing when topics are meaningful
and connected to real-life experiences. This chapter offers suggestions for organizing and teaching
students authentic writing for publication. Subjects
include choosing writing topics, using mini-
lessons, developing independent writing skills,
coordinating writing with other phases of the publishing process, and conducting conferences.

TIME FRAME

Topic selections **1 day**
Writing articles **3–4 days**
Adding illustrations **3–4 days**

Getting Started

Use reproducibles and mini-lessons to teach students different writing techniques. Help them brainstorm and organize their ideas before writing their articles. Offer guidance, encouragement, and support as students express their thoughts and ideas aloud and on paper.

Magazine Title and Theme

Invite students to brainstorm and vote on a title and theme for your class magazine. Some theme ideas may include seasons (articles relating to the current season), science fiction, sports, or school events.

Topic Selection

Invite students to choose topics to write about, such as friendship, dogs, or baseball. Model how to narrow the topic selection and brainstorm facts to include in the article. For example, a student choosing to write an article on friendship may narrow the selection to "Ten Ways to Create the Perfect Friendship" and brainstorm a list of pointers.

For students having difficulty generating topic ideas, suggest articles linked with personal experiences or subjects being studied in class. For example, while studying biographies in literature, have students interview and write classmate biographies. Explain that writers are given assignments geared toward the needs of a certain publication.

Choosing a Format

After students have decided on writing topics, have them select article formats and record their choices on their Writer's Report (page 119). Discuss with students how appealing, successful magazines contain articles that vary in both content and style. Have student pairs look through children's magazines and list the kinds of articles found. Discuss how articles can be grouped into categories by format (e.g., advertisements, cartoons, movie reviews). Invite students to brainstorm possible writing formats while you list their ideas on chart paper. Display this master list in the classroom throughout the writing process, and make copies for students to refer to in their writing folders.

Article Formats

Use this article format list to assist students as they brainstorm their own, or copy and distribute the list below to promote class discussion.

SONGS

contests

crafts

cartoons

advice columns

book reviews

GAMES AND PUZZLES

interviews

HOW-TO ARTICLES

fictional stories

biographies

POETRY

jokes and riddles

wish lists

OPINION LETTERS

ADVERTISEMENTS

crossword puzzles

movie reviews

quizzes

information articles
(sports, school events, animals, travel)

experiments

RECIPES

plays

Writing Articles for Publication

The flexibility of magazine publishing makes it adaptable to all ability levels. Apprehensive writers may start with short pieces (jokes or comic strips), then move on to writing full-length articles. After students complete one type of writing, have them choose another. Students may complete only one writing piece per format (e.g., one poem).

Mini-Lessons

Use mini-lessons (pages 49–72) to teach specific writing skills. Conduct mini-lessons with the whole class or in small groups once or twice a week. Add your own mini-lessons as you evaluate and adjust curriculum to meet your students' needs.

Choose mini-lessons based on your grade-level objectives and student abilities. Depending on students' needs, you may choose to spend more time reinforcing certain writing concepts. Provide opportunities for students to apply their new skills as they write magazine articles.

Illustrations

Allot one writing period each week for students to illustrate their work. Setting aside specific time for illustration eliminates students turning daily writing time into drawing time.

Most illustrations should be black and white unless you are using a color copier to print magazine pages. You may wish to have students make drawings a particular size to fit the magazine format, or simply use a copy machine to make the adjustments. Ask students to first make sketches using pencil on plain white paper. Have students wishing to submit illustrations for publication trace over them with a black felt-tip pen.

Student Conferences

The information you gain discussing a student's writing helps you assess student needs and plan future writing lessons. During conferences, ask students to tell you about their writing—verbalizing ideas helps students see things from different perspectives and invites them to try new approaches. Be careful not to edit at this time; rather, tell students what you find interesting about their writing, and invite them to expand on those points.

To obtain the most information, ask students open-ended questions such as:

- *What are you working on today?*
- *Could you read it to me?*
- *I really like the part where . . .*
- *What are you most proud of?*
- *Was there anything difficult about writing this piece?*
- *What did you do about this problem?*
- *May I give you an idea to help the next time you have this problem?*
- *Do you feel it is ready to submit for our next publication? Why or why not?*

Management

Conferencing can be conducted individually or in small groups. The key to successful conferencing is to set realistic goals for yourself—it is not necessary to meet with every student each week. Conferencing with one or two students a day, three to four days a week, is sufficient. By meeting with just a few students a week, you will accumulate more pertinent information than if you sat down and graded a pile of their writing samples.

It is critical that students are occupied with independent work while you meet with others for training and conferencing. Always include additional activities for students who complete work early. Encourage students to ask classmates for help before interrupting conferences, or have them work on other assignments until you are free to assist them. Invite students to brainstorm a list of rules to follow during writing periods. Write their ideas on chart paper, and post them in a prominent place. Rules may include:

- Use your time wisely.
- Everyone writes during writing time.
- If you get stuck, put that piece aside and start a new one.
- Ask your classmates for help when the teacher is unavailable.
- Use your quiet voice when speaking to others.
- Never throw any writing away—keep lists of ideas, rough drafts and final pieces in your writing folder.

Teaching Tips

- Have partners of different ability levels write articles together.
- Have students share their stories orally—to another student or into a tape recorder—before writing their ideas on paper.
- Provide many opportunities for students to share work in progress with classmates. Have students share "cliff-hangers," inviting classmates to suggest how stories should end.
- Have each student list goals at the beginning of each writing period, then check goals off as they are completed. This is a valuable management tool to use while you conduct student conferences.
- Invite students to create computer-generated illustrations.
- Invite parent volunteers to assist students with writing while you conduct conferences.
- Keep your eyes open for writing contests offered by various publications and invite students to participate.

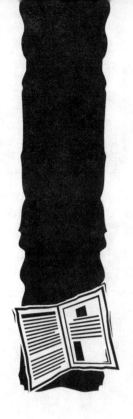

Students as Editors

After writing for three to four weeks, students are now ready to work as class editors. This chapter provides helpful suggestions for teaching students to self- and peer-edit, including tips on using reproducible materials, conducting practice sessions, and managing students as they rotate from one editor to the next.

TIME FRAME

Training to self-edit **1–2 days**

Peer-editing review **1 day**

Editing papers—students **1–2 weeks**

Editing papers—teacher **2–3 days**

Self-Editing

Students develop independence, proficiency, and self-awareness about their writing skills as they self-edit work. Use reproducible sheets and the Editing Techniques mini-lesson (page 52) to introduce editing marks and show students how to edit work. Repeat instruction throughout the year as needed.

Materials

Provide students with the following reproducibles to use with mini-lessons and throughout the self-editing process.

- Editing Guide (page 86)—Introduces a list of conventional editing marks. Students keep this sheet in their writing folder for reference when self- or peer-editing.

- Self-Editing Guide (page 99)—Lists questions to guide students as they self-check their work. Students will need a new copy of this guide each time they self-edit their writing.

- Class Training Samples (pages 100–101)—Provides unedited writing samples for students to edit and revise. These are only used with teacher supervision during class or small-group editing sessions.

- Revising Checklist (page 102)—Offers revising guidelines for sequencing, paragraph structure, and sentence clarity. Students will need a new copy of this checklist each time they self-edit their writing.

- Editor Sign-Off Sheet (page 103)—Staple to papers after self-editing is complete. These sheets are signed by classmates during peer-editing.

Developing Self-Editing Skills

Have students practice editing skills with training samples before editing their own work. Ask each student to choose one or two samples from his or her writing folder to self-edit and submit for peer-editing, revising, and publication. Have students use the Self-Editing Guide, Editing Guide, and the Revising Checklist to self-edit and revise their own writing.

At the beginning of the year, you will notice some students finish quickly, making very few marks on their papers. As skill levels improve, students become more proficient at identifying and correcting errors.

After students have completed self-editing, have them staple an Editor Sign-Off Sheet to their revised papers for peer editors. You may wish to collect writing pieces at this time to evaluate and guide students' self-editing techniques.

Peer-Editing

Peer-editing helps students develop proficiency in writing, cooperation skills, and appreciation for other writing styles. Student editors use the Editing Guide (page 86), Editors' Checklists (pages 87–90), and information from training sessions (see *Training Staff*, pages 27–28) to edit others' work.

The Rotation Process

Each editor wears a name tag to designate which job he or she holds—Art, Capitalization, Content, Cover, Distribution, Layout, Punctuation, or Spelling Editor. (Even though Art, Cover, Distribution, and Layout Editors are not editing at this stage, they should wear name tags to show they are part of the publishing workforce.) Students also display desk plates to indicate they are available for peer-editing. Color-code and laminate checklists, name tags, and desk plates to organize and reuse materials.

Authors are not assigned to specific editors. However, each author is responsible for meeting with one Capitalization, Content, Punctuation, and Spelling Editor in a specified period of time (usually four or five days). Art, Cover, Distribution, and Layout Editors do not meet individually with students—they circulate their own papers for editing or work on new writing.

When students become authors, they circulate through the various editors and place their desk plates face down to indicate they are "out." If students cannot find an available editor, they return to their seats and work while they wait. A student may choose to lay a submission on the desk of an editor who is "out" to signal that he or she would like to meet with that editor.

When students act as editors, they stay at their seats with desk plates up to indicate they are "in" and able to edit a peer's paper. Editors may also circulate from student to student, offering editing assistance. (If they stay in their seats, editors can work on their writing in between editing sessions.)

Editors may only work with one author at a time. When editors are working with students, they place their desk plates down to indicate they are busy. Editors can use colored pens or pencils to make editing marks, and then discuss corrections with the author as they mark his or her work. After meeting with an author, each editor initials the Editor Sign-Off Sheet attached to the submission.

After each editor checks a writing piece, the author should return to his or her seat and make only the noted corrections before visiting the next editor. Students will recopy the entire piece just prior to publication, after it has been seen by four student editors (Capitalization, Content, Punctuation, and Spelling) and yourself (Senior Editor). Editors are not required to recheck papers after corrections have been made unless you feel this will make them more accountable.

Management

As Senior Editor and teacher, you monitor student performance and work quality. Circulate and offer assistance to students throughout the editorial process. Encourage students to self-edit carefully before submitting their work to peer editors. Expect some students to finish self-editing while others move on to peer-editing. Role-model rotation procedures and reinforce the importance of discussion between authors and editors. Explain to students that editing is not a race—in one class period they should meet with no more than two authors. Remind students to be considerate of those working independently. (You can designate a quiet work area away from peer-editing stations.) After peer-editing is complete, meet briefly with individual students to assist with final revisions. Use the Editor's Grade Sheet/Rubric (page 117) to assess and record student progress. See *Assessment and Evaluation* (pages 45–48) for further guidelines.

Teaching Tips

- Share examples of good student editing for motivation and encouragement.
- Have weekly class discussions to share feelings about how the program is progressing. Encourage students to share positive experiences and constructive comments, and ways their peers have been helpful and supportive.
- Share your own experiences with writing and revising papers—students appreciate the support and understanding you offer regarding the practice, patience, and time it takes to develop good writing skills.

Putting It All Together

After completing the editing process, students enter the most exciting phase of magazine publishing—bringing together writing, art, and design to create the final product. This chapter details how students complete final magazine production—conducting staff meetings, deciding layout of magazine articles and illustrations, creating the magazine cover, and printing final copies for distribution.

TIME FRAME

Magazine cover and interior layout **1–2 weeks**
Final revisions, printing, and distribution **4–5 days**
Post-production assessment and celebration **1 day**

Editorial Meetings

Have Art, Layout, Cover, and Distribution Editors meet while other students revise articles. Schedule meetings so no more than two groups meet simultaneously, providing all students time to revise articles, keeping noise level to a minimum.

Review classroom courtesies and guidelines for group behavior, encouraging students to respect others while they work. Discuss and model proper cooperative group behavior, giving all members the opportunity to share their ideas, listening respectfully to others, and finding peaceful ways to compromise when conflicts arise. You may choose to assign specific responsibilities and roles to each editorial group (leader, reporter, secretary, supplies manager) when holding staff meetings.

Layout Staff

Ask students to choose one or two pieces of edited and revised writing to submit to Layout Editors. If they decide to submit a cartoon, game, or puzzle, ask them to also submit a full-length article. If you see duplicate articles (such as ten book reviews), you may request new submissions or let the situation pass and discuss it during post-production evaluation.

During layout meetings, editors discuss and decide on magazine layout, taking into account article size and artwork, visual appeal, and available space on magazine pages. They look through and compare the layout of different children's magazines to brainstorm ideas for the class magazine.

When a layout has been decided, editors cut and paste articles and illustrations onto 11" x 18" butcher paper or poster board, forming a "dummy issue" for the entire class to discuss. (Students may find it helpful to draw columns on butcher paper pages, using restickable glue to position articles.)

When the mock-up is approved, Layout Editors lay out the actual magazine pages. They number the pages, add any necessary headings, and develop a table of contents before submitting it for printing and distribution.

LAYOUT EDITOR

Cover Staff

Cover Editors begin their first meeting with a private class vote to determine which article to feature on the front cover—have students submit two- to three- line summaries of their submitted articles for Cover Editors to share during the voting process. Then, editors decide on a four- to five-word "attention-grabbing" phrase to correlate with the featured article. Subsequent meetings focus on where the phrase will be placed on the cover, along with supportive artwork, the magazine title, date, and volume number.

Cover Editors also create an inside front cover, listing the names of magazine staff. Both the front and inside front cover are given to you with pages from the Layout Editors. (Note: The back cover of the magazine is reserved for addresses of magazine subscribers.)

Art Staff

During Art meetings, editors decide which writing pieces need illustrations and where to place them on magazine pages. They collect artwork that students have accumulated and saved from weekly art sessions, then choose which illustrations best fit the magazine. Art Editors may request additional illustrations, if needed.

Distribution Staff

Distribution Editors meet to tally subscription forms and see how many copies of the magazine are needed. When the magazine is published, Distribution Editors and student volunteers address the back covers. Have them formally address issues for students to share with their families (e.g., The Smith Family, 300 Main Street, Anytown, USA 22222).

Printing and Distribution

How you choose to print your magazine greatly depends on available resources. When printing the magazine cover, use a color printer or colored paper for the front and back covers. Laminate covers of classroom copies for durability. Remember, your magazine does not have to look perfect—imperfections can lead to valuable problem-solving experiences.

Magazine Publishing

Use the following suggestions to print the final copies of your magazine.

- If the issue is handwritten, Layout Editors can use students' final copies to make the "dummy issue" and then use this to make multiple copies. It may be helpful to use a copy machine to reduce article size before creating the "dummy issue."

- Student or parent volunteers can type articles on typewriters or computers during computer laboratory time. If necessary, down-size pages on the copier to fit the original layout. Have Layout Editors cut and paste the pages again to make an 8½" x 11" "dummy issue," then print multiple copies on a copy machine.

- If you have access to a computer with a newsletter format, the entire issue can be typed exactly as originally laid out. Leave room for illustrations and print multiple copies on a copy machine.

Magazine Distribution

After final issues are run, the entire class assists in collating and stapling copies. Place a stack of each page on separate desks, in sequence—students can walk around the class picking up pages from the stacks, collating and stapling them together.

As students finish final production, Distribution Editors address back covers, then distribute magazines to in-school subscribers. Other students may assist labeling and delivering magazines, if needed. Students hand deliver magazines to their families and other subscribing friends.

Management

At the beginning of each writing period, list on the chalkboard both individual and group goals. Students can refer to this list to monitor their own progress. While most students are writing final copies, you can meet separately with Art, Cover, Layout, and Distribution Editors to assess and guide their progress. Between conference sessions, circulate and monitor students working independently.

Final Production Schedule

Monday
- All students work on final copies.
- Teacher monitors and checks progress as students work.

Tuesday
- Layout Editors read submitted articles to determine which will appear in the magazine.
- Art Editors look at submitted illustrations to determine which will appear in the magazine.
- Cover Editors meet to narrow down articles that may be featured on the cover.
- Students work on final copies of their submissions.

Wednesday
- Layout Editors receive some final copies from students. They categorize articles and determine page layouts.
- Art Editors make final decisions about which articles will include artwork.
- Other students work on final copies or begin a piece (student-selected or assigned topic) for the next magazine.

Thursday
- Art Editors make final decisions regarding artwork.
- Layout Editors receive final articles. They make a mock-up for classmates to review and approve.
- Cover Editors take a vote to decide which article should be featured on the cover. They meet to decide on a four- or five-word catchy phrase for the cover. They also determine whether to use clip art, computer-generated pictures, or ask the author of the feature article to submit (or choose) an illustration for the cover.
- Distribution Editors tally subscription forms to see how many copies are needed.
- Other students work on final copies, articles for the next magazine, or assist Distribution and Layout Editors.

Friday
- Layout Editors complete page layouts, organizing (cutting and pasting) all pieces and sequencing pages for the final magazine.
- Cover Editors make final decisions regarding the cover.
- Other students work on final copies, articles for the next magazine, or assist Layout Editors.
- Parent volunteers print magazine pages for students to collate and distribute the following week.

Post Production

After publishing each magazine, watch students beam with pride when they see their articles in print. Have students assess and evaluate their experiences, for both staff effort and magazine content. Afterward, have a post-production party and invite students to share their contributions with the class.

Performance Evaluation

Self-assessment is important to students' writing development. Have students assess and evaluate the overall success of magazine publishing. Ask students to suggest possible solutions or improvements for the next magazine issue, including types of articles they would like to see. Discussion questions may include:

- *What was done well during the publication process? Did the class work as a team? Were editors constructive?*
- *What do you think about the magazine overall? Did it offer a good assortment of articles?*
- *What can be done to improve the next issue?*

Recognitions and Rewards

The class party is a good time to present special student rewards. Be sure to recognize and reward each student for their contributions. Recognitions and rewards include:

- Editors' Paychecks (page 123)—Graded performance based on participation in magazine publishing.
- Special Recognition Award (page 124)—Use this award to recognize each child's special contribution to the publishing process.
- Teamwork Award (page 125)—Awarded to students for good team spirit.
- Certificate of Achievement for Cover Story (page 126)—Recognizes the author of the article featured on the front cover.
- Employee of the Month Certificate (page 127)—Recognizes one or more individuals who have been exceptional contributors to the publishing process.

Teaching Tips

- Assign a parent volunteer to each editorial group to assist students.
- Invite Art, Layout, and Cover Editors to share progress with classmates during class discussions.
- To reduce layout time, give groups of three or four students a page to lay out. Layout Editors can then add final details (page numbers, table of contents) before submitting it for printing.

Assessment and Evaluation

This chapter offers a variety of evaluation methods

to assess and evaluate student performance. Use

these tools to determine students' strengths and

weaknesses and to monitor achievement through-

out the writing program. Evaluation and assessment

of student performance may also be used to guide

lesson planning for subsequent magazine issues.

Assessing Student Performance

Use the following reproducibles to assess student progress at regular intervals throughout the publishing process. Use a binder with tabs to organize and store teacher records. Create writing portfolios to store evaluations and copies of student work. Allocate your time in advance—prepare a schedule to observe and record progress of specific students each week.

Interest Survey

Administer Interest Surveys (pages 80–81) at the beginning of your program to determine the writing attitudes, interests, and experiences of your students. This helps in planning your program, selecting topics, and allocating jobs. Store the surveys in student portfolios. Distribute the survey again at the end of the program and compare student responses.

Anecdotal Records

Make copies of the Anecdotal Records (page 114) to record and date observations about students' writing attitudes, strengths, weaknesses, and conferencing sessions. Circulate freely while students write, observing where they are in their writing. Look for examples of students using strategies effectively in their work and praise these examples, perhaps sharing them with the class before noting them in your records. File these observation sheets in your Teacher Records binder, and use them as documentation for grading and commenting on student performance.

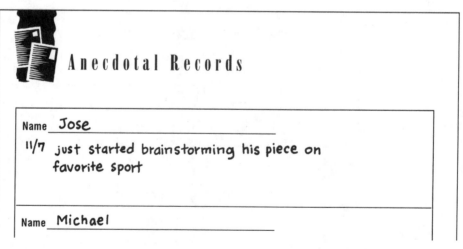

Anecdotal Records

Name __Jose__

11/7 just started brainstorming his piece on
        favorite sport

Name __Michael__

Writing Assessment

Use Writing Assessments (page 115) to evaluate students' writing samples. Have students select one or two pieces for you to evaluate. Fill out and attach assessment sheets to student writing samples. Place a "yes" or "no" in each blank, or assign each question a number value to determine student grades—remember to check your anecdotal records as you answer the questions. Have students complete self-assessments (page 120) for each submitted sample, then conference with students to compare responses. Send evaluated work

home for parents and students to review together. Have both parents and students sign evaluation sheets before returning them to you. Store assessments and copies of student work in writing portfolios.

Student Editor Positions

To help track the jobs each student performs throughout the year, use the Student Editor Positions chart (page 116). With this record, you can track student jobs to ensure they occupy a variety of publishing positions.

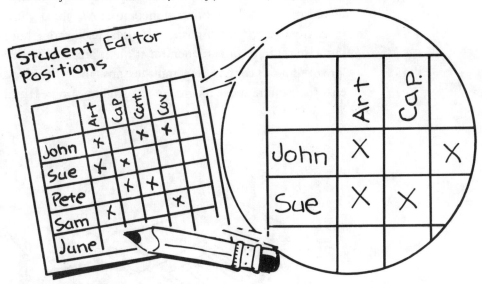

Editor's Grade Sheet/Rubrics

Use the appropriate Editor's Grade Sheet/Rubric (page 117) to evaluate the job performance of each Content, Spelling, Punctuation, and Capitalization Editor. Make two copies of each record—one for student writing folders and the other for student portfolios. Use these evaluations to share findings with individual editors and record student job performance. You may choose to decide grades for "paychecks" and Employee of the Month selections based on these evaluations.

Mini-Lessons

Use anecdotal records, reproducibles, and writing pieces to record, grade, and evaluate student performance and the effectiveness of mini-lesson instruction. You may also plan the objectives and activities of subsequent mini-lessons based on this assessment.

Writer Evaluation

Use Writer Evaluations (page 118) at the end of magazine publishing to assess each student's overall writing skills. Store these evaluations in your Teacher Records binder, and refer to them as you determine final writing grades.

Student Self-Evaluation

Have students use the following reproducibles to self-assess and record their progress. Refer to these self-evaluation sheets when meeting with students or conferencing with their parents. Watch students become more responsible, accountable, and successful in writing as they monitor and critique their own work.

Writer's Report

Have students keep their Writer's Reports (page 119) in writing folders to record writing skills (editing, punctuation, vocabulary usage) and formats (interviews, advice columns, crosswords) used throughout magazine publishing. Use these records to monitor student progress and determine objectives for subsequent conferences, mini-lessons, and writing exercises. Invite parents to examine these records to see student progress and skills being taught.

Writer's Self-Assessment

Have each student complete a Writer's Self-Assessment (page 120) when submitting a sample for teacher evaluation. Provide the reproducible Good Writers Use . . . (page 121) to guide students as they assess and evaluate their work.

Workshop Assessment

Review and discuss skills learned at the end of magazine publishing. Have students complete What I Learned About Magazine Publishing (page 122) as an assessment tool. You may choose to have students list or summarize additional knowledge about magazine publishing on the back of the reproducible, or invite students to create their own cloze activities for classmates to complete. Store the review sheets in student portfolios.

Mini-Lessons

This chapter contains mini-lessons that teach skills using different writing formats. All lessons incorporate teacher modeling, cooperative learning, and analyzing authentic writing samples. Each lesson has been classroom tested and requires little preparation time. Teach one or two mini-lessons each week with your whole class (unless otherwise specified). Choose lesson topics as they arise or apply lessons according to your specific skills objectives. Adapt these lessons to your needs or use them as springboards for your own lessons. After teaching a mini-lesson, have students add the writing skill or format to their Writer's Report. Students can use this information to monitor their work and develop responsibility.

Mini-Lesson 1: Nouns and Adjectives

Objectives

Identify nouns.

Define a noun as a person, place, or thing.

List nouns related to various seasons.

List adjectives that describe nouns and use them in holiday stories.

Materials

Seasonal Sort (page 104)

Seasonal Sort transparency

overhead projector

overhead markers

pencils or pens

Procedure

Day One

1 Brainstorm a list of people, places, and things associated with the fall season. Write student ideas on the chalkboard.

2 Explain to students that all words listed on the board are nouns—people, places, or things. Write this definition above the list, and place the Seasonal Sort transparency on the overhead projector.

3 Give each student a copy of Seasonal Sort, and ask him or her to copy "place" words from the board next to the schoolhouse, "people" words next to the boy, and "thing" words next to the crayon.

4 Ask students to think of a describing word (adjective) that would help others visualize each person, place, or thing, then write the adjective in front of each noun. For example, if a student wrote the word *apple* in the "thing" list, he or she may choose to add the word *juicy* in front of it.

Day Two
Have students use corrected sheets as story starters to write about fall. Ask them to use their word pairs in their stories. Explain that the previous day's lesson was another way to brainstorm ideas.

Teaching Tips

- Have students write noun-adjective pairs for other seasons (spring, summer, and winter).
- Extend learning by adding verbs to word groupings.
- Have students write definitions and sample words for different parts of speech and keep them in writing folders for reference.
- Have students identify parts of speech in student dictionaries (see *Mini-lesson 5: Dictionary Skills*).

Mini-Lesson 2: Editing Techniques

Objectives

Apply editing techniques to written material.
Revise written material for content and clarity.

Materials

Editing Guide (page 86)
samples of unedited work
overhead projector
overhead markers
unedited work transparency
pens, colored pencils, or crayons

Procedure

1 Share the Editing Guide with students and explain editing marks.

2 Display a transparency of an unedited work sample. If using student work, always ask first, delete the name, and compliment the author for strengths in the piece.

3 Model editing, reading through the entire sample at least once before starting. Only edit for one thing at a time and color-code editing marks to make them easier to see. (For example, red for punctuation and green for spelling.)

4 Assign students to groups of four. Give each group a copy of a new sample of unedited writing. All groups should have the same sample.

5 Ask each student per group to use a different colored pen, pencil, or crayon to edit the sample for one skill area—capitalization, content, punctuation, or spelling.

6 Meet back with the entire class and edit the same piece, one skill area at a time. Note parts that seem unclear and discuss how they might be revised.

Teaching Tips

- Advise students to self-edit work at least one day after initial writing is complete to ensure a "fresh look."
- Advise authors to make corrections to their writing immediately after editing while their memory is clear.

Mini-Lesson 3: Parts of Speech

Objectives

Identify parts of speech.
Eliminate overused words.

Materials

writing paper
pencils or pens

Procedure

1 After a lesson on parts of speech, such as verbs, nouns, or adjectives, help students devise a contest to reinforce each skill. Contest outlines should include: guidelines, rules, deadline date, someone to which entries should be returned, and prize.

2 Encourage students to work with partners and share their ideas. They can also exchange contests and complete them for homework.

THE AWESOME ADJECTIVE CONTEST

Guidelines: See how many adjectives you can find that begin with the letter A.

Rules: You must work independently.

Deadline: October 7

Return Entries to: Sara Lu

Prize: Free homework pass

Teaching Tips

- Extend this idea to include other parts of speech. This approach also works great with overused words. For example, have a Scintillating Synonym Contest—see how many synonyms students can find for the overused words *good*, *nice*, and *big*.
- Students can use these guidelines to develop and submit their own contests for publication in subsequent magazines. One magazine issue can contain the contest guidelines and the next announce the winners.
- If students from other classes participate in the contests, enlist the support of fellow teachers to distribute free homework passes or other rewards to winners.

Mini-Lesson 4: Commas

Objective

Identify and use commas correctly.

Materials

    copies of children's magazine article
    Comma Quest reproducible (page 105)
    highlighter or colored pens
    scissors
    glue

Procedure

1 Distribute article copies to students. Have them read the assigned story silently, then read it aloud as a class.

2 Tell students they are going on a punctuation "treasure hunt" called Comma Quest. Ask students to find all the commas in the article and highlight or underline entire sentences where punctuation is found.

3 Choose a few students to copy sentences on the board. Elicit an explanation from the class as to why each comma was used.

4 Discuss the use of commas
- in a series.
- to separate compound sentences.
- when using quotation marks.

5 Distribute Comma Quest sheets, and have students cut and paste sentences from their articles under the appropriate treasure chests. After checking for accuracy, ask students to place sheets in their writing folders for future reference.

Teaching Tip
- Teach commas over several lessons, focusing on each use separately before having students complete Comma Quest.

Mini-Lesson 5: Dictionary Skills

Objectives

Practice dictionary skills.
Create personal writing dictionaries.

Materials

Writing Dictionary reproducible (page 106)
8¹/₂" x 11" construction paper
scissors
staplers
dictionaries
student writing folders
pens, crayons, and markers

Procedure

1 Help students make Writing Dictionaries as follows:
- Make 13 copies of the Writing Dictionary reproducible for each student.
- Have students cut along the dotted lines to make two dictionary pages per reproducible sheet.
- Ask students to fold construction paper in half to create a cover.
- Staple pages inside the cover to make a book.
- Have students write letters *A–Z* sequentially on the top right corner of dictionary pages.
- Ask students to title the front cover *Writing Dictionary* and add their names at the bottom. Invite students to decorate their covers.

2 Ask students to choose five to ten words they have difficulty spelling from writing samples in their folders. If students are weak spellers, help them choose commonly-used words from their writing. If students are strong spellers, they can choose five to ten interesting or challenging words they would like to use in their writing.

3 Ask students to write chosen words on the correct page in their dictionary, and complete information about the word using class dictionaries—part of speech, number of syllables, and synonym or short definition.

4 Have students keep Writing Dictionaries in their writing folders for future reference. Set aside time each week for students to add words to their dictionaries, or have them add new words as needed.

Teaching Tips

- Have students use words from writing dictionaries for weekly spelling lists.
- Invite students to share writing dictionaries as they work on articles.

Mini-Lesson 6: Alliteration

Objective

Use alliteration effectively to develop headlines for stories or articles.

Materials

book featuring alliteration (e.g., *Six Sick Sheep* by Joanne Cole and Stephanie Calmenson, *Fast Freddie Frog* by Ennis Rees, *A Twister of Twists, a Tangler of Tongues* by Alvin Schwartz, or *Faint Frogs Feeling Feverish* by Lilian Obligado)

writing paper

pencils or pens

student writing folders

Procedure

1 Read to students from a book of alliteration. Explain alliteration and how it is formed.

2 Share how brainstorming is essential to good alliteration. Ask students to write down the name of an animal, then list adjectives that start with the same sound as the animal's name. Have them do the same with verbs, nouns, and adverbs. For example: *Pete's pet pig prefers pink pineapples.*

3 Using the following pattern, have students build their own alliteration about animals, using the pattern *adjective + adjective + noun (animal) + verb + adverb.* For example: *Seven silver swallows sang sweetly.*

4 Have students use words from favorite writing samples in their folders to create catchy alliterative headlines for magazine stories and articles.

Teaching Tips

- Use lengthier patterns for more advanced learners [e.g., *adjective (amount) + adjective + noun (animal) + verb + adverb*].
- Invite students to include illustrations with their alliterations.
- Have a tongue-twisting contest with student-generated alliterations.

Mini-Lesson 7: Vocabulary

Objectives

Define specific vocabulary words.
Correctly spell vocabulary words.
Use vocabulary words in context.

Materials

overhead transparencies
overhead markers
graph paper
science textbooks
writing paper
overhead projector
crayons or pens
dictionaries

Procedure

Day One

1 Before the lesson, make two transparencies of graph paper and one transparency with 10–15 vocabulary words copied from a science book. Prepare to discuss the meaning, spelling, and usage of each word.

2 Allow students to preview science material containing the selected vocabulary words. Ask student pairs to locate and list ten words they think are most important to the material.

3 Have students share their list orally with the class. Allow them to discuss why they chose particular words. Show them your list on the overhead projector to see how many of the same words were chosen.

4 Bring in crossword puzzles to share with students. Give each student two pieces of graph paper. Using the overhead projector, model how to intersect words on graph paper to form a crossword puzzle answer key— then trace the outline on a second sheet to create a blank puzzle for others to complete.

5 Have students choose eight to ten of the words to make a crossword puzzle. Have them number each of their words from the top of the page to the bottom and trace the used boxes with a dark crayon or pen. Explain that if two words intersect at their starting letters, one will be down and one across.

6 Have students place their other piece of graph paper over the answer key. Ask them to trace the dark outlines and number the beginning space of each box in the upper left corner.

7 Have students use dictionaries to write definitions or fill-in-the-blank clues for each word below the puzzle and number the definitions and clues to correspond with puzzle numbers. (Make sure students understand how to separate the down and across clues.)

Day Two

1 Select and copy student crossword puzzles not intended for magazine submissions.

2 Distribute crosswords to student partners and invite them to solve the puzzles.

Teaching Tips

- Invite students to create crossword puzzles using vocabulary words from other subject areas.
- Have students complete crossword puzzles at home with their families.
- Invite students to create other writing activities to reinforce vocabulary such as word searches, fill-in-the-blank stories, and clue games (written clues to identify a secret word).

Mini-Lesson 8: Summarizing Ideas

Objective

Summarize reading selections.

Materials

novel or story students previously read

videotape of a Reading Rainbow episode (Lancit Media Productions, New York)

children's magazine book corner section

Book Review Summary reproducible (page 107)

Procedure

1 Have students view and analyze book talks of a Reading Rainbow episode. Ask them to share ways the book reviews stimulate interest and motivate children to read the books.

2 Show students the book corner section of a children's magazine. These examples are usually very short, focusing on the main theme and highlights of each reviewed book. Discuss the purpose of the section with students, and have them compare the video and magazine book reviews for content and style.

3 Have students complete Book Review Summaries, then use them to write one-paragraph book reviews. Invite students to read their reviews to the class.

Teaching Tips

- Add student pictures to published book reviews.
- Use movie reviews to practice summarizing skills.

Mini-Lesson 9: Writing Directions

Objective

Write multiple-step directions.

Materials

classroom objects (paper clips, erasers, pencils)
instructions from science experiment, craft project, or math problem
writing paper
pencils or pens

Procedure

1 Have one student wait outside the classroom while another hides a small object inside. Invite the student back inside and have others verbally guide him or her to the hidden object. Emphasize the importance of clear, precise, and accurate directions.

2 Share aloud craft instructions, a science experiment, or math problem to illustrate how directions are written. Have students write an explanation of each step and ask partners to compare steps. Invite students to share their work with the class. Discuss how there is a variety of ways to give directions, emphasizing that they must be clear and sequential. Point out that illustrations can also be helpful.

3 Have students write "how-to" articles about a favorite hobby for magazine submissions or portfolios.

Teaching Tips

- Have students exchange "how-to" directions and complete the activity independently. Have them "star" when directions are clear and highlight when clarification is needed.
- Invite students to collect and share favorite "how-to" articles from children's magazines.

HOW TO PRINT YOUR OWN GREETING CARDS

Mini-Lesson 10: Supporting Details

Objective

Write sentences with supporting details.

Materials

Be a Detail Detective reproducible (page 108)
chart paper
marker
pencils or pens
encyclopedias
reference books on animals

Procedure

1 Provide each small group of students with a Be a Detail Detective sheet. This sheet lists three sentences with main ideas about three animals (frogs, pandas, and dinosaurs). For example: *Frogs are amphibians.*

2 Challenge groups to find one fact about each animal on their sheet that supports the main idea sentence. For example: *Frogs have lungs.* Then ask students to use each fact in a detailed sentence. All groups should end up with three animal facts and three detailed sentences.

3 Invite groups to share their sentences with the class. Write them on chart paper under main idea sentences.

Teaching Tips

- Have student use these facts to write animal stories for publication.
- Invite students to write new main idea sentences and have partners add supportive details.
- Invite parents to write main idea sentences about family trips and have students add supportive details.

Mini-Lesson 11: Writing Dialogue

Objectives

Write dialogue between two characters.
Use quotation marks properly in dialogue.

Materials

magazine or newspaper comic strips
overhead transparencies
overhead projector
overhead markers
writing paper
Create-a-Comic reproducible (page 109)
pencils or pens

Procedure

1 Make two or three overhead transparencies or photocopies of favorite comic strips. Use these to model how to rewrite dialogue from comic strips with quotation marks.

2 Give student pairs a comic strip. Have each student choose one of the characters and rewrite the dialogue using quotation marks.

3 Distribute Create-a-Comic sheets, and have students develop their own comic strip.

Teaching Tips

- Invite students to listen to dialogue from video- or audio-taped television shows and write the dialogue on paper.
- Invite more advanced students to write scripts to share with classmates.

Mini-Lesson 12: Informative Letters

Objectives

Review material relevant to content areas such as science, social studies, and health.
Practice letter writing.
Use reference materials to locate information.

Materials

reference materials (encyclopedias, textbooks, nonfiction books)
index cards
art supplies
index card container
writing paper
pencils or pens

Procedure

1 Discuss with students that many children's magazines have columns to which children can write and ask questions. (For example, the "Ask Scarlett" column in *Ranger Rick*.)

2 Develop your own "Ask . . . " column around a particular unit you are studying, such as ocean life, rain forests, or fitness. Have each student generate one or two questions on your topic to write on index cards.

3 Place all cards in a container and have each student pull one or two cards. Have them use appropriate resources to search for and write answers to the questions.

Teaching Tip

- If students can't find answers, refer them to your media specialist or consider sending unanswered questions to a publication—they may answer one in an upcoming issue.

Mini-Lesson 13: Advice Letters

Objectives

Write advice letters using correct letter form.
Use problem-solving strategies to answer advice letters.

Materials

newspaper or magazine advice column
writing paper
pencils or pens

Procedure

Day One

1 Distribute copies of an advice column. Discuss content and article format.

2 Have students write a "Dear (use your magazine or mascot name)" letter, asking advice about a problem they have. Ask students to avoid being too personal or mentioning names. Review correct letter form—date, greeting, body, closing, and signature. Collect letters for Day Two.

Day Two

1 Choose four or five letters and make five copies of each.

2 Introduce problem-solving strategies.

> **Problem-Solving Strategies**
> Identify the specific problem.
> Brainstorm ideas to solve the problem.
> Discuss the pros and cons of each solution.
> Choose a solution to write.
> Implement the solution and evaluate the success.

3 Divide students into groups of four or five. Give each group an advice letter and choose one member from each group to record ideas. Have students devise solutions and write them in response form.

4 Discuss problems and advice as a class. Choose letters to submit to the next edition of the magazine.

Teaching Tip

- Invite students from other classes to submit questions for your students to answer.

Mini-Lesson 14: Surveys

Objectives

Use proper form to develop letters.
Write addresses properly on envelopes.
Collect and analyze data.
Display data appropriately using a graph.

Materials

newspaper or magazine survey or Interest Survey (pages 80–81)
chart paper
marker
8½" x 11" paper
business envelopes (four per student)
scissors
writing paper
pencils or pens

Procedure

Day One

1 Display a survey to students. Explain that surveys compare and rate how people feel about a selected topic. Write four animal names across the top of the board. Ask students to come up and write their names under their favorite animal. Tally each column, summarize the class survey, and discuss results.

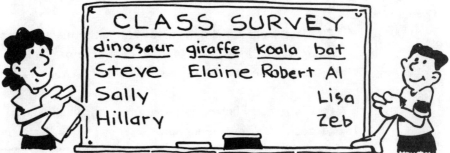

2 Ask students for other possible survey topics. Help students understand that surveys can be as simple as your animal survey or much more involved.

3 Tell students they are going to develop and administer (as a class) a survey on a topic of their choice. They will report the information in the form of a graph in the next magazine issue.

4 Brainstorm survey topics such as favorite things (animals, sports, breakfast cereals), political views, change of a law or rule, or fitness issues. Remind students to keep ideas relevant to their readers.

5 After choosing a topic, have students respond to the following questions:
- *Who will take your survey?*
- *How many will take your survey?*
- *How many questions will you include in your survey?*
- *How will you distribute your survey?*

6 On chart paper, write a class cover letter to accompany each survey. Model proper letter structure—date, greeting, body, closing, and signature. Make sure the letter introduces your class, explains the purpose of the survey, and requests assistance.

Day Two

1 Now students are ready to develop their survey. Ask them to keep it simple so more people are likely to respond. How students distribute their survey depends on the topic. If an in-school postal system or in-school E-mail system is available, surveys can be sent to other students. If not, consider the following ideas:
- A survey on school policies sent to all local principals, school board members, or PTA members.
- A student survey sent to random households in the neighborhood.
- A student survey sent to family members out of state. (Students can bring in addresses. Or, if you have a friend or family member who teaches in another state, consider sending them a class set of surveys.)

2 After deciding who to survey and gathering addresses, model how to properly address envelopes. Cut a piece of blank 8½" x 11" paper in half lengthwise (mock business envelope) for each student.

3 Write the following information on the chalkboard for students to practice addressing envelopes.

FROM
_____
_____
_____

TO
Joel Montel
634 Lockspoint Road
Anytown, Virginia 02332

4 When students can properly address envelopes, give them real business envelopes to address. Make sure to send enough surveys so everyone has the opportunity to address at least two envelopes. Remember, each outgoing envelope needs a self-addressed stamped envelope for returned surveys.

5 Ask students to each bring in four stamps, enough for two surveys each. If that is not feasible, ask for school or PTA funds to help with the project. As an alternative, use postcards for surveys, as they require less postage. If you have an in-school postal system, you will only need to provide envelopes.

6 Tally the data as surveys return. Determine how students report this information in the next magazine issue. Students can analyze the data and report information in terms of fractions and percentages.

Teaching Tip

- As an extension, invite students to publish a survey in the magazine and report the results in the following issue.

Mini-Lesson 15: Biographies

Objectives

Interview someone to obtain information.
Write an article that answers the questions who, what, when, *and* where.
Use information obtained in an interview to write biographical sketches.

Materials

magazine article (biography or interview)
Interview Outline reproducible (page 110)
writing paper
pencils or pens

Procedure

1 Read the article aloud to students. Discuss valuable contributions children and adults have made to society. *National Geographic World* has a column titled "Kids Did It," featuring children who have done special or exciting things.

2 Ask students to interview children or adults in your school. Have them choose individuals who have done something special (winning an award, traveling to a foreign country), or invite students to interview a best friend, teacher, principal, librarian, or other school employee.

3 Explain that "reporters" must always have questions prepared, and organize an interview place and time. Have students write questions on Interview Outlines, and arrange a meeting time and place for their interviews. Encourage students to ask open-ended questions such as *Where were you born? What is your favorite childhood memory?*

4 Invite students to conduct interviews, then record answers in the form of a biography. For added fun, invite "reporters" to tape-record responses, and use the tape to help write their biographies.

Teaching Tip

- Integrate this lesson with topics in science, health, or social studies by having students focus on famous explorers or scientists.

Mini-Lesson 16: Advertisements

Objectives

Write advertisements using vivid and precise language.
Practice using the thesaurus.

Materials

magazine or newspaper advertisements
thesauruses
art supplies

Procedure

1 Have students study various advertisements and list the major components of each. Discuss similarities and differences in slogans, logos, short descriptive sentences, and eye-catching pictures.

2 Invite students to circle words which may be too general or overused in the advertisements. Have them use thesauruses to find more vivid and precise words, or add their own pertinent details to the advertisements. New words must have the same connotation as the originals.

3 Ask students to develop advertisements of their own. Invite them to write ads for services available at your school, such as:
- cafeteria
- school store
- in-school postal delivery
- upcoming events
- student government fund-raisers
- library
- "accelerated reader" program

Teaching Tip

- Have students view and analyze television commercials to generate more ideas. Invite them to share their findings with the class.

Mini-Lesson 17: Persuasive Writing

Objective

Write a persuasive piece using supporting details to convince readers.

Materials

    toy
    newspaper and magazine editorials
    writing paper
    pencils or pens
    Persuasive Writing Outline reproducible (page 111)

Procedure

Day One

1 Begin the lesson with the following role-playing situation.

- Choose a student to be a "store clerk" and explain that you will be the "customer" interested in purchasing a toy.
- Tell the store clerk you plan on going to several stores to shop around. It is the store clerk's job to convince you to purchase the item at this store.
- Remind the store clerk to focus on the product and not become too forceful. He or she must be able to support claims with relevant details or you may choose to shop elsewhere.
- While role playing is going on, involve other students by having them jot down supporting details the clerk uses to persuade you.

2 After the skit, discuss the relevance and effectiveness of the store clerk's reasoning. Point out that in order for persuasion to be effective, it must be:

- Backed by specific concrete information.
- Relevant to the reader.
- Presented clearly.

3 Read aloud and discuss editorials from newspapers and magazines. Evaluate them according to the standards listed in step 2.

Day Two

1 Provide students with a Persuasive Writing Outline to help them organize their ideas and prepare a persuasive writing piece. Work through each section with students—choosing one idea each student feels strongly about, listing reasons supporting this viewpoint, planning attention-grabbing introductory sentences, writing sentences to counter possible objections, and providing convincing conclusions.

2 Invite students to share their persuasive writing with classmates.

Persuasive Writing Outline

Name ___Julie___ Date ___11/28___

Think of three things you feel very strongly about or would like to see changed. These ideas could relate to any aspect of your life, such as school, home, friends, or the environment. Write your ideas in complete sentences.

I think we should have a longer lunch break.

I don't think that hunting should be legal.

I don't think kids should have a curfew.

Choose one idea to develop further. Choose one you can support with specific details. On the lines below, list as many reasons as you can think of to support your feelings and opinions.

- Waiting in line for hot lunch takes too much time.
- By the time we sit down with our lunches, there's only about 15 minutes left to eat our food. That's not good for digestion.

Teaching Tips

- Before sharing their speeches aloud, have students brainstorm possible objections, then decide how they will counter the objections to prove their points.
- Have students write persuasive speeches for a class debate. Choose a topic relevant to your students' interests, such as school uniforms, curfews, and gun control.

Mini-Lesson 18: Poetry

Objective

Create different forms of poetry.

Materials

Me Poem reproducible (page 112)
Writing Poetry reproducible (page 113)
writing paper
pencils or pens

Procedure

Day One

1 Seat students in a circle and give each a copy of the Me Poem. Have students take turns completing a line. This activity helps students see how simple poetry can be, as well as how diversity makes poetry come alive.

2 Create other round-robin poetry using synonyms, antonyms, "crunchy" words, "itchy" words, sad words, words that start with a particular letter, one-syllable words, "soft" words, words that describe your best friend, seasonal words, and "tasty" words. Students will be excited and motivated to develop poems with all these great words.

Day Two

1 Share the four different poetry formats from the Writing Poetry sheet—Haiku, Diamonte, Cinquain, and Shape poems.

2 In small groups or with partners, have students create poems based on these models (one poem per group). Invite students to share their poems with the class.

Teaching Tips

- If the class doesn't see how a student's choice fits into the poem, wait until the round is done and ask the student to explain his or her response. It then becomes a wonderful lesson on differing perspectives.
- Have students keep the Writing Poetry sheet in their writing folders for reference.
- Share good poetry (patterned or unpatterned) with students on a regular basis.

Reproducibles

The reproducible pages provided in this chapter

make it easy to set up your "publishing house" and

teach the publishing process to your students.

Reproducibles are grouped into five categories—

Organization, Editing, Mini-Lessons, Teacher

Records, and Student Records and Rewards (see

footer at the bottom of each page). Before begin-

ning a lesson, check which reproducibles you

need and make copies.

Name Tags

Capitalization Editor

_____
Name

Art Editor

_____
Name

Cover Editor

_____
Name

Content Editor

_____
Name

Senior Editor

_____
Name

Write to Publish © 1996 Creative Teaching Press

Name Tags

Distribution Editor

_____
Name

Layout Editor

_____
Name

Punctuation Editor

_____
Name

_____
Name

Spelling Editor

_____
Name

Desk Plates

Capitalization Editor

Art Editor

Desk Plates

Content Editor

Cover Editor

Desk Plates

Distribution Editor

Layout Editor

Desk Plates

Punctuation Editor

Spelling Editor

Interest Survey

Name _____ Date _____

Do you enjoy writing in school? Why or why not?

_____

_____

_____

_____

_____

_____

What are some of the topics you have written about?

_____

_____

_____

_____

_____

_____

Do you prefer to choose your own topics or have topics assigned to you? Why?

_____

_____

_____

_____

_____

_____

Write to Publish © 1996 Creative Teaching Press

Have you ever published your writing in a class book or magazine? If so, how did you feel about it?

_____

_____

_____

_____

_____

What do you consider your biggest strength in writing?

_____

_____

_____

_____

_____

What writing skill would you like to improve?

_____

_____

_____

_____

_____

Would you like to have your work published in a class magazine for others at school and home to see? Why or why not?

_____

_____

_____

_____

_____

Job Descriptions

Art Editor
- Decides which articles will be accompanied by pictures.
- Chooses pictures to be published.

Capitalization Editor
- Checks writing for correct use of capital letters.
- Refers writers to the class English text for reference.

Content Editor
- Works with writers to assure writing is clear.
- Helps writers add interesting details.
- Praises writers for writing that is clear, expressive, or exciting.
- Checks to see that details are in the proper order.

Cover Editor
- Decides artwork for cover.
- Chooses headline for cover.
- Sets up cover for final print.

Distribution Editor
- Distributes subscription order forms.
- Tallies subscription orders.
- Makes master list of customers.
- Writes addresses on the backs of magazines.
- Delivers magazines.

Layout Editor
- Arranges and pastes articles and illustrations in the magazine.
- Helps make decisions regarding the number of pages and columns.

Punctuation Editor
- Checks to see if end marks are used correctly.
- Checks to see if each paragraph is properly indented.
- Checks for proper use of quotation marks and commas.
- Refers writers to the class English text for reference.

Spelling Editor
- Checks writing for spelling errors.
- Circles errors.
- Assists writers with dictionary and thesaurus use.

Senior Editor (Teacher)
- Interviews and trains students for their jobs.
- Circulates, supervises, monitors, and conferences with student writers and editors.
- Makes the final edit of the magazine.
- Evaluates writers and editors when the magazine is finished.

Write to Publish © 1996 Creative Teaching Press

Job Application

for _____ **Publishing House**

Please print all information clearly.

Name _____

Date of Birth _____

Address _____

_____

Phone Number _____

For which positions are you applying? (check two)

_____ Art Editor

_____ Capitalization Editor

_____ Content Editor

_____ Cover Editor

_____ Distribution Editor

_____ Layout Editor

_____ Punctuation Editor

_____ Spelling Editor

Please describe your qualifications below. What makes you the best person for the job? (You may want to refer to the job descriptions before you begin.)

_____

_____

_____

_____

_____

Job Contract

_____ **Publishing House**

I, _____, promise to carry out my duties as

_____ to the best of my ability. I will

support my fellow writers, follow daily writing rules, and contribute my

own material to each issue.

Signed _____

Date _____

Signature of Senior Editor _____

Subscription Order Form

Dear Reader,

The next issue of _____, a magazine by the students of

_____, will be available soon. If you would like to receive a

complimentary copy for your classroom library, please complete the subscription

request form below, and return it to Room _____.

_____ Yes! I would like to receive the next edition of your classroom magazine.

Name _____

Address/Room # _____

_____

✄ --

Subscription Order Form

Dear Reader,

The next issue of _____, a magazine by the students of

_____, will be available soon. If you would like to receive a

complimentary copy for your classroom library, please complete the subscription

request form below, and return it to Room _____.

_____ Yes! I would like to receive the next edition of your classroom magazine.

Name _____

Address/Room # _____

_____

Editing Guide

Name _____   Date _____

Correction	Symbol	Example
lowercase	/lc	She took her Dog for a walk.
capitalize	≡	tom went to the party.
delete	e	Alice jumped over over the log.
misspelled word	⬭	Can you cach the ball?
new paragraph	�	After eating dinner, John went to sleep. The next day, John rode his bike to school.
add/insert	∧	We had fun at the carnival.
move	↶⬭	Juan found at the park his ball.
insert missing punctuation	◯	Travis said, "Wow! What a game."

Write to Publish © 1996 Creative Teaching Press

Capitalization Editor's Checklist

❶ Have the author read the article to you.

❷ Read the article silently.

(Ask the author to wait quietly while you read.)

❸ Read the article aloud again. As you read, ask yourself these questions:

- Did the author capitalize the first letter of each new sentence?

- Did the author capitalize all proper nouns (names of people and places)?

- Did the author capitalize days of the week and months of the year?

- Did the author capitalize "I" when it stood alone?

- Did the author capitalize the titles of books and movies?

- Did the author capitalize titles of people, such as Mr., Mrs., Ms., and Miss?

❹ Use proper editing marks to correct any capitalization errors you find. Discuss these corrections with the author.

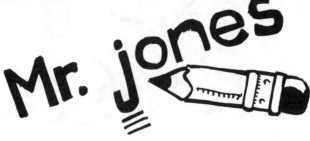

Content Editor's Checklist

❶ Have the author read the article to you.

❷ Read the article silently.

(Ask the author to wait quietly while you read.)

❸ Read the article aloud again. As you read, ask yourself these questions:

- What do you really like about the piece?

- Were there any parts you found confusing?

- Was the piece written in a logical order?

- Could more detail be added at any point within the piece?

- Were there any overused words?

- Did the piece have a beginning, middle, and end (conclusion)?

❹ Discuss your answers to the above questions with the author.

Write to Publish © 1996 Creative Teaching Press

Punctuation Editor's Checklist

❶ Have the author read the article to you.

❷ Read the article silently.

(Ask the author to wait quietly while you read.)

❸ Read the article aloud again. As you read, ask yourself these questions:

- Are there periods at the end of all statements?

- Are there question marks at the end of all questions?
  (Look for words like *who, what, where, why,* and *when.*)

- Are exclamation points used properly?

- Are commas used in compound sentences as needed?

- Are commas used properly in lists? in dates?

- Are all paragraphs indented?

- Are quotation marks used around direct words of a speaker?

- Are commas used to separate the speaker's words from the speaker's name?

❹ Use proper editing marks to correct any punctuation errors you find.
Discuss these corrections with the author.

Spelling Editor's Checklist

❶ Have the author read the article to you.

❷ Read the article silently.

(Ask the author to wait quietly while you read.)

❸ Read the article aloud again.

❹ As you read, circle any possible misspelled words.

❺ Discuss these words with the author.

❻ Do not correct the author's spelling errors. Suggest the author look up all questionable words in the dictionary.

Write to Publish © 1996 Creative Teaching Press

Training Sample for Capitalization Editors

Name _____   Date _____

Using the appropriate editing marks and your Editor's Checklist, edit the following paragraph for capitalization only. On the back of this page, write compliments you would give this author.

Reading Adventures

if you are thinking about reading a good book and aren't sure which one to choose, you may want to try one of these. james and the giant peach is a funny adventure story by roald dahl. in this story, james escapes from his two mean aunts, aunt sponge and aunt spiker, and travels in a runaway giant peach. if you like adventures with a scary twist, you may like terror at the zoo by peg kerret. A brother and sister spend the night in a local zoo and are confronted by a criminal on the loose. A great adventure story with a fantasy twist is elizabeth winthrop's the castle in the attic. your public library is full of wonderful books like these. stop by and have your own adventure in reading.

Training Sample for Capitalization Editors
● Answer Sheet ●

Reading Adventures

if you are thinking about reading a good book and aren't sure which one to choose, you

may want to try one of these. james and the giant peach is a funny adventure story by

roald dahl. in this story, james escapes from his two mean aunts, aunt sponge and aunt

spiker, and travels in a runaway giant peach. if you like adventures with a scary twist,

you may like terror at the zoo by peg kerret. A brother and sister spend the night in a

local zoo and are confronted by a criminal on the loose. A great adventure story with a

fantasy twist is elizabeth winthrop's the castle in the attic. your public library is full of

wonderful books like these. stop by and have your own adventure in reading.

Write to Publish © 1996 Creative Teaching Press

Training Sample for Content Editors

Name _____ Date _____

Using the appropriate editing marks and your Editor's Checklist, edit the following paragraph for content only. On the bottom of this page write two compliments you would give this author and two suggestions for improvement.

My Trip to the Museum

Last week I went to a museum. It was very interesting. I saw dinosaur bones and fish.

The tour guide told us about the history of many animals. I saw animal footprints, too. It was exciting.

Compliments:_____
_____
_____
_____
_____

Suggestions: _____
_____
_____
_____

Training Sample for Content Editors
• Answer Sheet •

My Trip to the Museum

Last week I went to a museum. It was very interesting. I saw dinosaur bones and fish.

The tour guide told us about the history of many animals. I saw animal footprints, too. It

was exciting.

Possible compliments:

❶ I like your choice for an article topic.

❷ I like that you have a clear beginning and end to your paragraph.

❸ I like that you mention several things you saw at the museum.

Possible suggestions:

❶ Include the name and location of the museum.

❷ Use more descriptive words (adjectives and adverbs) to describe more clearly what you saw.

❸ Include more specific information that you learned from the tour guide—which animals were discussed, historical facts you learned.

❹ The sentence about animal footprints seems out of place. Move it next to other sentences describing what you saw at the museum.

Write to Publish © 1996 Creative Teaching Press

Training Sample for Punctuation Editors

Name _____ Date _____

Using the appropriate editing marks and your Editor's Checklist, edit the following paragraph for punctuation only. On the back of this page write compliments you would give this author.

How to Grow a Sunflower

Do you know how to grow a sunflower All you need is a sunflower seed a cup of soil,

water and sun. Fill the cup half full with soil Use a pencil to poke a hole in the bottom

of the cup to drain excess water. Push the seed into the cup of dirt place in sunlight,

and water every other day. Soon you'll be saying, "Wow Look at my beautiful sunflower

Training Sample for Punctuation Editors
● Answer Sheet ●

How to Grow a Sunflower

Do you know how to grow a sunflower? All you need is a sunflower seed, a cup of soil,

water, and sun. Fill the cup half full with soil. Use a pencil to poke a hole in the bottom of

the cup to drain excess water. Push the seed into the cup of dirt, place in sunlight, and

water every other day. Soon you'll be saying, "Wow! Look at my beautiful sunflower."

Write to Publish © 1996 Creative Teaching Press

Training Sample for Spelling Editors

Name _____   Date _____

Using the appropriate editing marks and your Editor's Checklist, edit the following word list for spelling only. On the back of this page write compliments you would give this author.

Winter Fun Word Search

The folowing is a list uf wrds that you will find hidden in this winter fun word search.

Thy may be writtn vertikally, horizontaly, or diagoneally. Helpfull hint: After you sircle each word in the puzzle, cross of the word form the list. Good luk!

snowbal   hot chawkolit

miten   snowflacke

sled   fireplase

skiing   eer muffs

koat   snownam

snowmobile   chille

Training Sample for Spelling Editors
• Answer Sheet •

Winter Fun Word Search

The following is a list of words that you will find hidden in this winter fun word search.

They may be written vertically, horizontaly, or diagoneally. Helpfull hint: After you sircle

each word in the puzzle, cross of the word form the list. Good luck!

snowball   hot chawkolit

miten   snowflacke

sled   fireplase

skiing   eer muffs

koat   snowman

snowmobile   chile

Write to Publish © 1996 Creative Teaching Press

Self-Editing Guide

Name _____ Date _____

❶ Did I use capitals properly?   Yes_____ No_____
  beginning of sentences
  title
  proper nouns
  I

❷ Did I circle all possible misspelled words?   Yes_____ No_____

❸ Did I check the spelling of these words in the dictionary?   Yes_____ No_____

❹ Did I use proper end punctuation?   Yes_____ No_____

❺ Did I use complete sentences?   Yes_____ No_____

❻ Did I use commas where needed?   Yes_____ No_____

❼ Did I underline overused or nonspecific words?   Yes_____ No_____

❽ Did I use the thesaurus to find more precise words?   Yes_____ No_____

❾ Did I indent each new paragraph?   Yes_____ No_____

❿ Is my writing easy to understand?   Yes_____ No_____

⓫ Did I use enough interesting details to support my ideas?   Yes_____ No_____

Class Training Samples

Name _____ Date _____

Use the correct marks to edit these paragraphs for capitalization, content, punctuation, and spelling. Then rewrite them on another piece of paper.

Sample 1

last week we went ot the norfolk zoo we were on a field trip it was a sunny daiy and we got to eet lunch in the park there were many different kinds of animals at the zoo mrs jones the anumal trainer taught us manye important facts about the animals we saw my favorite animal was the tier he had colorful stripes all over his entire body and he looked very sofft i don't think he is quite as cuddly as he looks i hope we will visit the zoo again soon

Sample 2

the story begins in the year 2782 on planet saturn millionare tyro peters from poland has travld their to join one millin other humins prior to coming to pluto tyro ran into some troble as he climed in the shuttle an evil-looking man tackled mr smith and mr. smith quickly got away and let the cops handle it after the man was taken to jail mr peters reumed his trip. Check out the next edition of the hammerhead to find out what Tyro plans to do on mars and why the mysterious stranger was after him.

Write to Publish © 1996 Creative Teaching Press

Class Training Samples

• Answer Sheet •

Use these corrected training samples to check your work. Spelling and punctuation corrections are in bold. Note that the content of your paragraphs may be slightly different.

Sample 1

Last week**,** we went on a field trip **to** the **N**orfolk **Z**oo**.** There were many different kinds of animals. I saw furry lions, funny monkeys, huge hippos, and tall giraffes. **M**y favorite animal was the ti**g**er**.** **H**e had colorful stripes all over his entire body and he looked very so**ft.** **I** don't think he is quite as cuddly as he looks**.** **M**rs**.** **J**ones**,** the animal trainer**,** taught us man**y** important facts about animals. Did you know that bears hibernate in the winter? It was fun seeing all the animals at the zoo. **I** hope we visit the zoo again soon**.**

Sample 2

The story begins in the year 2878. Millionaire **T**yro **P**eters from **P**oland is on his way to Saturn to join one milli**o**n other hum**a**ns. While boarding the shuttle, he runs into some tro**u**ble. An evil-looking stranger tackles Tyro and tries to stop him from boarding. Tyro quickly cries for help and the police arrive. They arrest the stranger and take him away in the police vehicle. But on the way to jail, he gets away! Meanwhile, Tyro boards the shuttle and continues his journey. But why is Tyro traveling to **S**aturn? Will the evil stranger try to stop Tyro again? Check out the next edition of **H**ammerhead Magazine to read more about Tyro's adventure and discover why the mysterious stranger is after him.

Revising Checklist

Name _____ Date _____

Find a favorite section in your writing. Think about why this part stands out from the rest, then answer the following questions.

- Does the item have an introduction? _____ body? _____ conclusion? _____

- Check the order. Are there any sentences or sections that need to be moved in order for the piece to flow better or make more sense? _____

- Look at paragraph structure. Is your writing piece one long paragraph? _____ Could it be separated into more than one paragraph? _____ Mark where you think the piece should be divided.

- Are there any parts you have a question about or seem confusing? _____

- Are there any sections that need a little more detail? _____ Mark these sections with a ☆.

Now go back and use the above suggestions to revise your work.

Write to Publish © 1996 Creative Teaching Press

Editor Sign-Off Sheet

Name _____   Date _____

Article Format (Category) _____

Title of Article _____

Have each editor initial below after editing your article.

<u>Initials</u>

Capitalization Editor   _____

Content Editor   _____

Punctuation Editor   _____

Spelling Editor   _____

Senior Editor   _____

Seasonal Sort

Name _____   Date _____

Person

Place

Thing

Write to Publish © 1996 Creative Teaching Press

Comma Quest

Name _____   Date _____

Find and highlight all sentences in your article that contain commas. Cut and paste each
under the correct treasure chest. Next, write your own sentences beneath each chest.
Use commas in each sentence to match the format used for each chest.

Writing Dictionary

My Guess	Dictionary Spelling	Part of Speech	No. of Syllables	Synonyms or Short Definitions

My Guess	Dictionary Spelling	Part of Speech	No. of Syllables	Synonyms or Short Definitions

Write to Publish © 1996 Creative Teaching Press

Book Review Summary

Name _____   Date _____

Book Title _____

In one sentence, describe what this book or story was about.

_____

Who or what did the story focus on? _____

Where and when did the story take place? _____

_____

Write one sentence about the most important event in the:

Beginning _____

_____

Middle _____

_____

End _____

_____

Did you enjoy the book? Why or why not? _____

_____

_____

_____

Be a Detective

Name _____   Date _____

Using available resources, find one fact about each animal that supports the main idea sentence. Place that fact in a detailed sentence.

Main Idea: Frogs are amphibians.

Fact: _____

_____

Detailed Sentence: _____

_____

_____

Main Idea: Pandas are interesting animals.

Fact: _____

_____

Detailed Sentence: _____

_____

_____

Main Idea: Some dinosaurs were carnivores.

Fact: _____

_____

Detailed Sentence: _____

_____

_____

Write to Publish © 1996 Creative Teaching Press

Create-a-Comic

Name _____   Date _____

Who are your two characters?

_____   _____

What will they say to one another?

Example: Joe said, "I found a lucky penny."
               "Where?" asked Mike.

_____

_____

_____

_____

_____

_____

Illustrate your comic. Include speech bubbles.

Interview Outline

Reporter's Name _____

I am interviewing _____

I chose to interview this person because _____

_____

_____

_____

_____

Questions I would like to ask him or her:

_____

_____

_____

_____

_____

_____

_____

_____

Note: Write answers to these questions on another sheet of paper.

Write to Publish © 1996 Creative Teaching Press

Persuasive Writing Outline

Name _____   Date _____

Think of three things you feel very strongly about or would like to see changed. These ideas could relate to any aspect of your life, such as school, home, friends, or the environment. Write your ideas in complete sentences.

_____

_____

_____

Choose one idea to develop further. Choose one you can support with specific details. On the lines below, list as many reasons as you can think of to support your feelings and opinions.

_____

_____

_____

Think of a way to grab your readers' attention and get them interested in your topic. Write one or more introductory sentences below.

Think of possible comments your readers may have and address them positively.

_____

_____

_____

Lastly, think of how to conclude your persuasive piece. Remember, you want to leave the reader as convinced as possible or at least considering your ideas. Caution: If you are too strong or critical you may scare the reader off.

_____

_____

_____

Write to Publish © 1996 Creative Teaching Press

Me Poem

Name _____ Date _____

I am _____

I am not _____

I like _____

I dislike _____

I laugh when _____

I cry when _____

I have _____

I have never _____

Someday I will _____

Write to Publish © 1996 Creative Teaching Press

Writing Poetry

Name _____   Date _____

Haiku, Cinquain, Diamonte, and Shape poems are fun ways to write poetry. Try your hand at creating your own poems.

Haiku

line 1—five syllables

line 2—seven syllables

line 3—five syllables

Cinquain

line 1—one word (two syllables)

line 2—description of subject (four syllables or two words)

line 3—feeling phrase (six syllables or three words)

line 4—feeling phrase (eight syllables or four words)

line 5—renaming subject (two syllables or one word)

Diamonte

one noun

two adjectives

three verbs

four nouns

three verbs

two adjectives

one noun

Shape poem

Anecdotal Records

Name _____

Name _____

Name _____

Name _____

Name _____

Teacher Notes:

- Always date comments.
- Record notes about academic performance and peer interactions. Take notes during conferencing and while students work independently.

Writing Assessment

Student Name _____ Date _____

Student followed steps for:

Brainstorming _____

Rough Draft _____

Editing Checklist _____

Final Copy _____

Student used:

Clear, easy-to-follow language _____

Supporting details _____

Logical sequencing of facts and ideas _____

An introduction _____

A conclusion _____

Correct capitalization _____

Good use of punctuation _____

Correct spelling _____

Teacher Comments:

_____

_____

_____

Parent's Signature _____

Student's Signature _____

Comments:

_____

_____

_____

_____

Student Editor Positions

Student Names	Art	Capitalization	Content	Cover	Distribution	Layout	Punctuation	Spelling

Write to Publish © 1996 Creative Teaching Press

Editor's Grade Sheet/Rubric

Content Editor

Editor's Name _____ Date _____

I have reviewed _____ (# of) pieces on which you signed off as Content Editor.

❹ You gave many accurate, positive comments and suggestions.
❸ You gave a reasonable number of ideas for the author to use.
❷ You gave a few ideas to help the author but could be more diligent.
❶ It did not appear that you gave the author much input to improve his or her piece.

Comments:

_____

_____

✂ -

Spelling, Punctuation, or Capitalization Editor

Editor's Name _____ Date _____

I have reviewed _____ (# of) pieces on which you signed off as
_____ Editor.

❹ You used many correctly placed editing marks.
❸ You used a reasonable amount of correctly placed editing marks.
❷ You used very few appropriate editing marks.
❶ You used too many or too few editing marks.

Comments:

_____

_____

Write to Publish © 1996 Creative Teaching Press

Writer Evaluation

Name _____   Date _____

❶ Writer makes good use of time. _____

❷ Writer produces a sufficient number of articles in the given time frame. _____

❸ Writer communicates ideas clearly through writing. _____

❹ Writer uses vivid and precise language in writing. _____

❺ Writer uses tools effectively (dictionary, thesaurus, reference materials). _____

❻ Writer uses correct self-editing techniques. _____

❼ Writer makes specified corrections after having an article edited. _____

❽ Writer is an effective peer editor. _____

❾ Writer keeps important materials organized in his or her writing folder. _____

❿ Writer has a positive attitude toward writing. _____

⓫ Editing jobs held to date: _____

_____

Overall evaluation: _____

_____

Write to Publish © 1996 Creative Teaching Press

Writer's Report

Name _____ Date _____

I was introduced to these writing formats. (Example: *"How to" articles*)	_____ _____ _____ _____ _____
I have used these writing formats.	_____ _____ _____ _____ _____

I was introduced to these writing skills. (Example: *Capitalize all proper nouns.*)	_____ _____ _____ _____ _____
I have used these writing skills.	_____ _____ _____ _____ _____

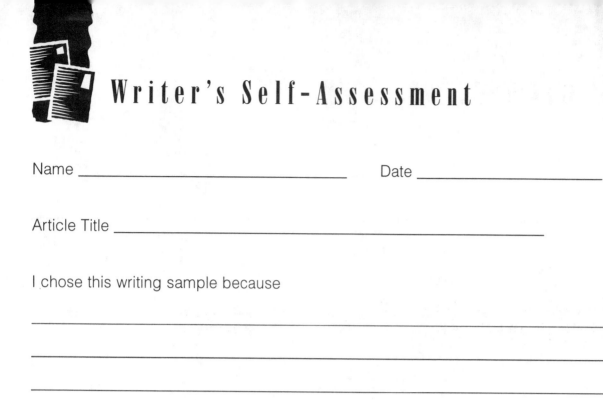

Writer's Self-Assessment

Name _____   Date _____

Article Title _____

I chose this writing sample because

_____

_____

_____

_____

_____

As I continue writing, I would like to improve the following skills:

_____

_____

_____

_____

_____

New writing formats I would like to try include:

_____

_____

_____

_____

_____

Capitalization

Complete Sentences

Original Ideas

CORRECT SPELLING

Punctuation

Vivid Language

Paragraphs

Complete Conclusions

Exciting Lead-ins

What I Learned About Magazine Publishing

Name _____   Date _____

Use the words in the box to complete the following paragraphs.

When you first sit down to write, it is important to get all your _____ on paper. You can do this by _____ or making a web. After you do this, you can begin your _____.

While writing, there are some workshop rules you need to remember. First, skip _____ so your writing will be easier to edit. Also, always put your name and the _____ on every piece. You should not worry about _____ at this point; just get your thoughts down on paper.

Next, look at the content of your writing to see if it makes sense and says everything you wanted to say. This step is called _____. You may add entire paragraphs or move sentences around. By doing this, you try to make the piece easier to _____. If your writing does not give enough information to support the main idea, you may need to add _____.

After you brainstorm, write your first copy, and check the content, it is time to _____. When looking for missing periods, commas, quotation marks, or question marks, we are editing for _____. When checking to see if uppercase letters are used properly, we are editing for _____.

Remember, the purpose of writing is to share your ideas with others in a way they can understand. Always use your time _____ and don't try to do everything at once. Knowing and using the steps to good writing can help you become a successful _____.

punctuation	lines	details	author	understand
ideas	edit	rough draft	revising	capitalization
date	spelling	wisely	brainstorming	

Write to Publish © 1996 Creative Teaching Press

Editors' Paychecks

_____ Publishing House

Date _____

Pay to the order of _____ Grade _____

For _____

Memo _____ _____
(Senior Editor's Signature)

_____ Publishing House

Date _____

Pay to the order of _____ Grade _____

For _____

Memo _____ _____
(Senior Editor's Signature)

_____ Publishing House

Date _____

Pay to the order of _____ Grade _____

For _____

Memo _____ _____
(Senior Editor's Signature)

Special Recognition Award

Awarded to _____

for _____

_____

_____

Congratulations for a job well done!

_____
(Senior Editor's signature)

_____
(date)

Teamwork Award

Awarded to _____

for excellent work as _____
(job title)

Thank you for being supportive and helpful to others.

_____
(Senior Editor's signature)

_____
(date)

Certificate of Achievement for Cover Story

This certifies that _____

had a story featured on the cover of _____ magazine.

Congratulations!

_____
(Senior Editor's signature)

_____
(date)

Employee of the Month Certificate

This certifies that _____ was chosen as Employee

of the Month at _____ Publishing House.

Congratulations for a job well done!

_____
(Senior Editor's signature)

_____
(date)

Appendix

American Girl

Pleasant Company Publications
8400 Fairway Place
Middletown, WI 53562

Biography Today

Omnigraphics, Inc.
Penobscot Building
Detroit, MI 48226

Boy's Life

1325 W. Walnut Hill Lane
P.O. Box 152079
Irving, TX 75015-2079

Highlights for Children

P.O. Box 182051
Columbus, OH 43218-2051

Kids Discover

170 Fifth Avenue, 6th Floor
New York, NY 10010

National Geographic World

National Geographic Society
P.O. Box 2330
Washington, DC 20078-9955

Ranger Rick

8925 Leesburg Pike
Vienna, VA 22184-0001

Sports Illustrated for Kids

Time Life Building
Rockefeller Center
New York, NY 10020-1393

3-2-1 Contact

E=MC Squared
P.O. Box 51177
Boulder, CO 80322-1177